For My Dear Friend,

With Love From

© 1999 Havoc Publishing
Artwork © 1999 Kathy Hatch

ISBN 0-7416-1119-8

Published by Havoc Publishing
San Diego, California

Made in China

All rights reserved.
No part of this publication may be reproduced or
transmitted in any form or by any means, electronic or
mechanical, including photocopying, recording, any
information storage and retrieval system without
permission in writing from the publisher.

www.havocpub.com

Havoc Publishing
9808 Waples Street
San Diego, California 92121

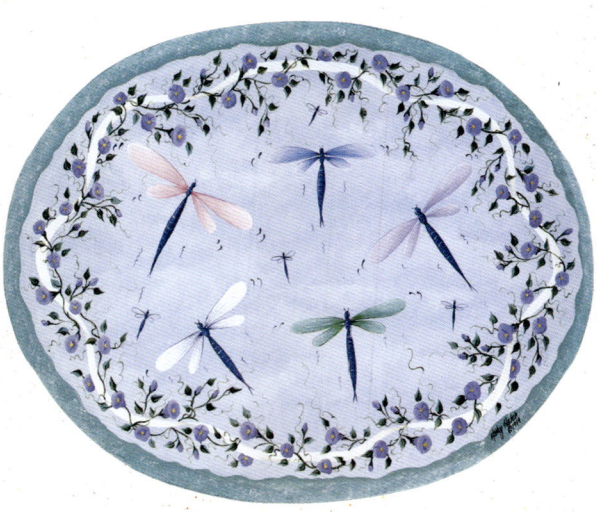

In the beauty of my garden
I sit and ponder
Why I have been blessed
With the love of a true friend.

Your friendship is a blessing
Like a garden filled with
flowers.
A day when nothing is
pressing
To sit with a friend and pass
the hours.

before you.
The indigo, this joyfulness
that's new.
The purple is the feelings our
friendship depends upon.
And at the end is a pot of gold
filled with affection!

Kindness in words creates confidence. Kindness in thinking creates profoundness. Kindness in giving creates love.

Lao-tsu

One who knows how to show and accept kindness will be a friend better than any possession.

Sophocles

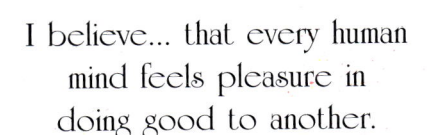

I believe... that every human mind feels pleasure in doing good to another.

Thomas Jefferson

Gratitude is the memory of the heart.

Jean Baptiste Massieu

The manner of giving is worth more than the gift.

Pierre Corneille

The best portion of a good man's life, his little, nameless unremembered acts of kindness and of love.

William Wordsworth

I count myself in nothing
else so happy as in a soul
remembering my
good friends.

William Shakespeare

If friends were flowers,
I'd pick you,
And how thankful I'd be
to find a friend like you.

Bees sip honey from flowers,
and hum their thanks as
they leave.
The gaudy butterfly is sure
that the flowers owe thanks
to him.

Rabindranath Tagore

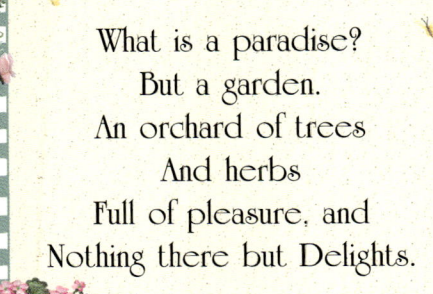

What is a paradise?
But a garden.
An orchard of trees
And herbs
Full of pleasure, and
Nothing there but Delights.

William Lawson

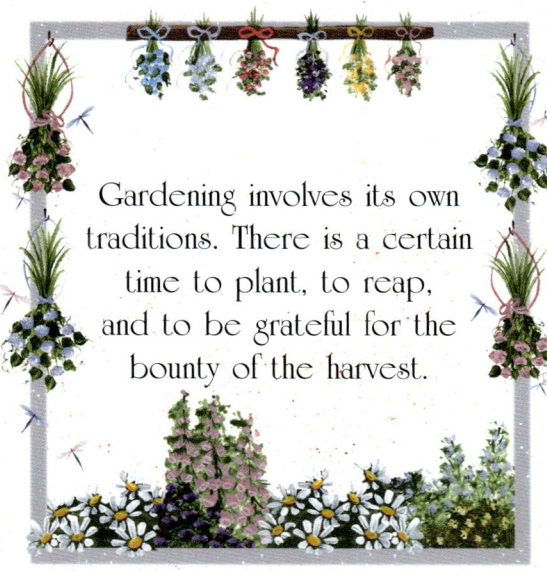

I am thankful for the sun, flowers
and the beauty that surround
me, but also for the love
of a friend.

Gardening touches all of
our senses.
To smell a flower's perfume,
To sit upon the benches,
To see the riot of colors of
the blooms,
All beautiful in their differences.

Nobody sees a flower—really—it's so small. It takes time—we haven't time—and to see takes time, like to have a friend takes time.

Georgia O'Keeffe

Our bodies are
our gardens,
to which our wills are
the gardeners.

William Shakespeare

> We do not see nature with our eyes, but with our understandings and our hearts.
>
> *William Hazlitt*

DRIED FLOWERS

HERBS

The day, water, sun, moon, night.
I do not have to purchase
these things with money.

Plautus

Nature never did betray
The heart that loved her.

William Wordsworth

There is that in the glance of a flower which may at times control the greatest of creation's braggart lords.

John Muir

> Reverence is one of the signs of strength; irreverence is one of the surest indications of weakness.
>
> *Anonymous*

To own a bit of ground,
to scratch it with a hoe,
to plant seeds, and watch
their renewal of life... this
is the commonest delight.

Charles Dudley Warner

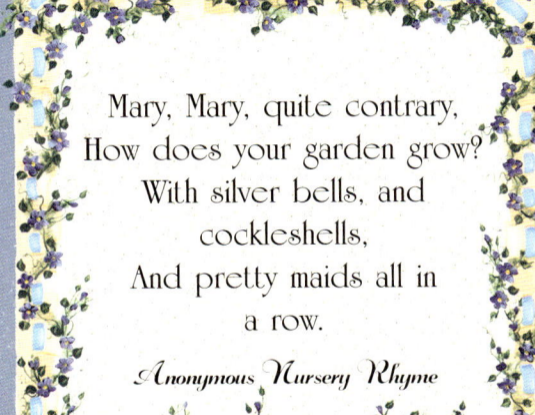

Mary, Mary, quite contrary,
How does your garden grow?
With silver bells, and
cockleshells,
And pretty maids all in
a row.

Anonymous Nursery Rhyme

What a man needs in gardening
is a cast-iron back,
with a hinge in it.

Charles Dudley Warner

A garden is a lovesome thing.

Thomas Edward Brown

I know a little garden close,
Set thick with lily and
red rose,
Where I might wander if
I might
From dewy morn to
dewy night.

William Morris

I should like to enjoy this summer flower by flower, as if it were to be the last one for me.

André Gide

I've often wish'd that I had clear,
For life, six hundred pounds a year;
A handsome house to lodge
a friend,
A river at my garden's end,
A terrace walk, and half a rood
Of land set out to plant a wood.

Alexander Pope

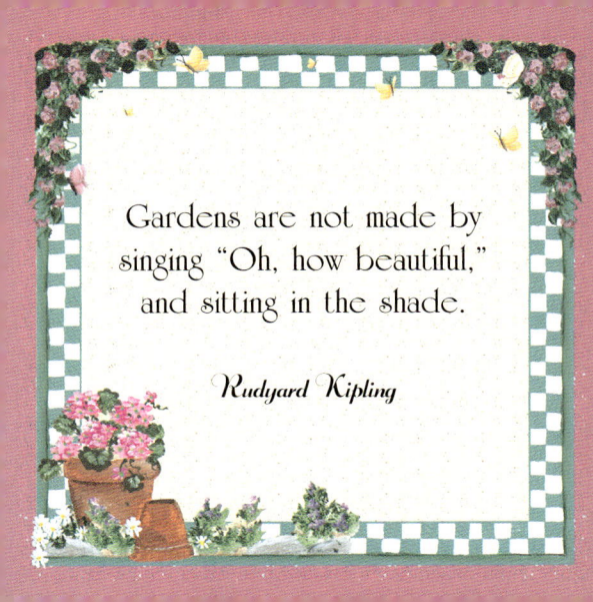

Gardens are not made by singing "Oh, how beautiful," and sitting in the shade.

Rudyard Kipling

Be thou the rainbow
to the storms of life!

Byron

No act of kindness,
no matter how small,
is ever wasted.

Aesop

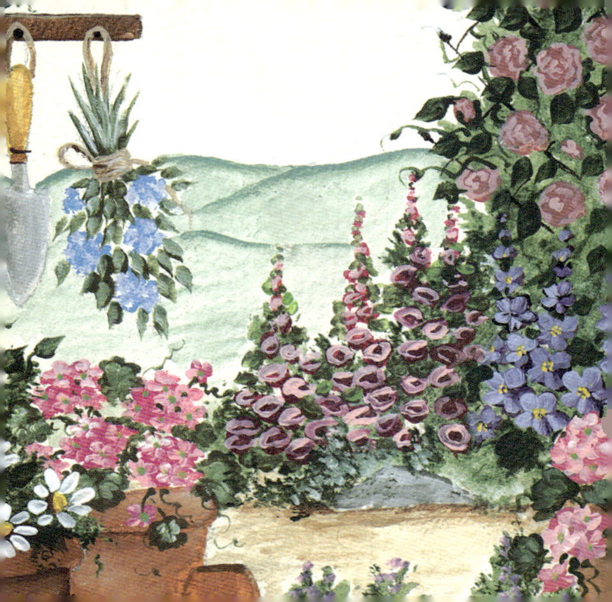

Now 'tis the spring, and weeds are shallow-rooted: Suffer them now, and they'll o'ergrow the garden.

William Shakespeare

A man of words
and not deeds
Is like a garden
full of weeds.

Anonymous Nursery Rhyme

A thing of beauty
is a joy forever.

John Keats

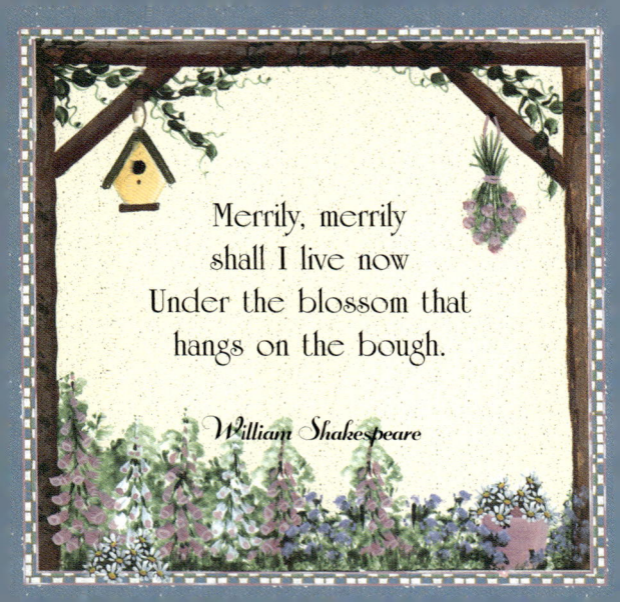

Merrily, merrily
shall I live now
Under the blossom that
hangs on the bough.

William Shakespeare

Sweet April showers
Do spring May flowers.

Thomas Tusser

Footfalls echo in the memory
Down the passage which we
did not take
Towards the door we never
opened
Into the rose garden.

T. S. Eliot

To Mercy, Pity, Peace
and Love,
All pray in their distress;
And to these virtues of
delight
Return their thankfulness.

William Blake

May I a small house
and a large garden have.

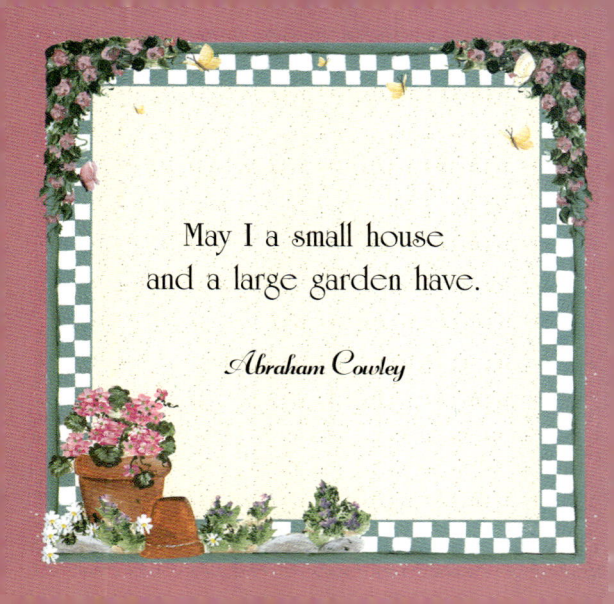

Abraham Cowley

If we stop to think of things important, we quickly realize those things aren't material; but they are the love, caring and sharing that come from others. These are the things that we should be thankful for.

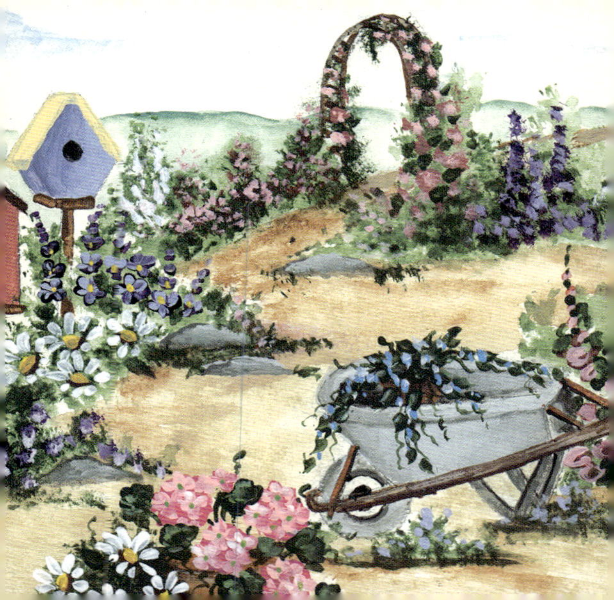

A garden is a place to stop and reflect, and appreciate all that nature has given us.

...half a proper
gardener's work
is done upon
his knees.

Rudyard Kipling

Oh, this is the joy of
the rose—
that it blooms and goes.

Willa Cather

And to give thanks is good,
And to forgive.

Algernon Charles Swinburne

Spring is never spring
unless it comes too soon.

G. K. Chesterton

A grateful mind
By owing owes not,
But still pays at once
Indebted and discharged.

Milton

Who bends a knee
when violets grow
A hundred secret things
shall know.

Rachel Field

> Why are there trees I never walk under but large and melodious thoughts descend upon me?
>
> *Walt Whitman*

Flowers and fruits
are always fit presents.

Ralph Waldo Emerson

WELCOME

Flowers leave some of their fragrance in the hand that bestowed them.

Chinese Proverb

Seeds of discouragement
will not grow
in a thankful heart.

Anonymous

There is nothing pleasanter than spading when the ground is soft and damp.

John Steinbeck

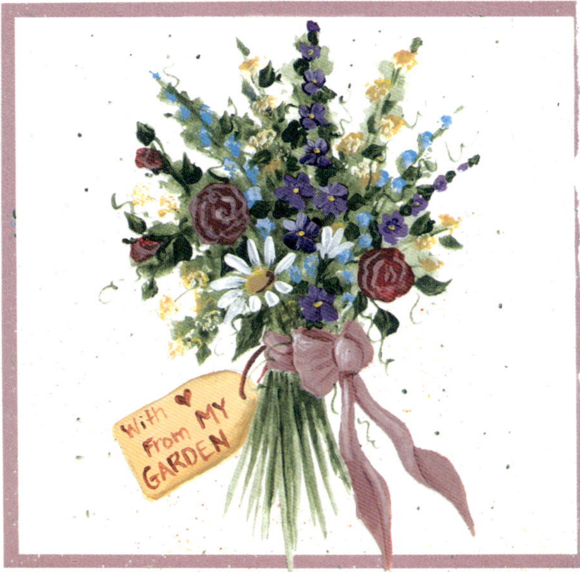
With ♥
From MY
GARDEN

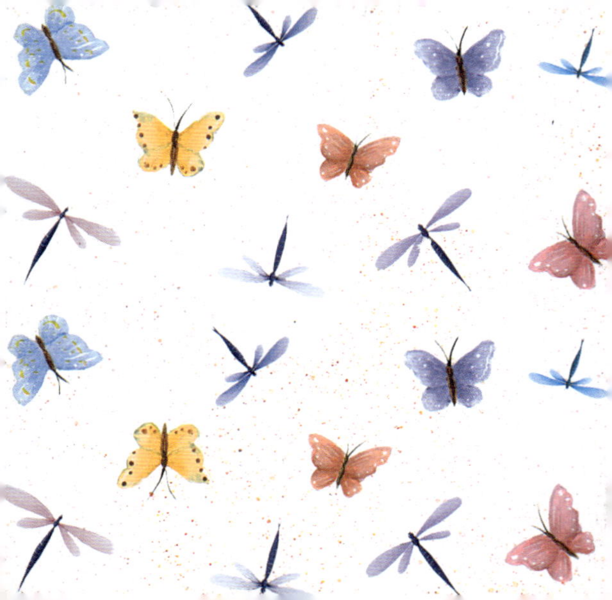